# THE SIX WIVES
## of
# HENRY VIII

*RIGHT:*
*It was imperative for Henry to ensure the continuity of the Tudor dynasty by producing a healthy legitimate male heir to succeed him. At a time when infant mortality was high and women were not expected to inherit the throne, Henry needed living sons.*

# Catherine of Aragon

BORN 1485, MARRIED 1509, DIVORCED 1533, DIED 1536

**H**enry's marital career began in the normal way for royal persons of his day. He was betrothed while still a boy to a girl-princess. The arrangements were handled exclusively by the parents on either side, and the main purpose of the marriage was to be diplomatic; to cement more firmly the alliance between the England of Henry VII and the Spain of Ferdinand and Isabella. The only slightly unusual feature was that Catherine of Aragon, the chosen bride, was already at the age of 17 the widow of Henry's elder brother, Arthur. Such impediment as might arise from this relationship was readily set aside by an edict of dispensation issued by Pope Julius II.

Catherine was born on 16 December 1485, the youngest of the five children of Ferdinand and Isabella who survived infancy, and almost immediately the bargaining for her hand began. By the time she was three she was betrothed to Arthur, Prince of Wales, who was not yet two. Naturally many years had to pass before the marriage could take place. At last, in 1501, shortly before her six-

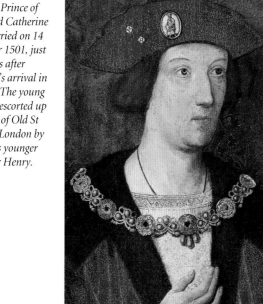

teenth birthday, Catherine made the storm voyage to England and was married t Arthur, now 14 years of age, within a few weeks. The young couple took up residence Ludlow on the Welsh border, but in less tha six months Arthur was dead. Never robu at the best of times he had succumbed t some infection which cannot now be pos tively identified.

Catherine's reaction to this sudden chang of fortune is not on record, nor do we real know how she had felt towards her sickl young husband, but in later years she persis tently maintained that their marriage ha never been consummated. Catherine's futur again lay in the hands of her parents and he father-in-law and their decision was that th Anglo-Spanish alliance must be maintaine and so, a little over fourteen months late she was betrothed to Arthur's younge brother, Henry. Catherine was now 17, bu Henry was under 12 and too young to marr for at least another two years. So once agai the wedding had to wait. This time, howeve all did not run quite so smoothly. By 150 King Henry VII was not quite so enthusiast about the Spanish alliance, and young Princ Henry, on attaining his fourteenth birthda was required by his father to repudiate h

bligations to Catherine on the grounds that hey had been entered into without his nowledge or consent. Catherine remained n England, but for the rest of Henry VII's eign her future was uncertain.

The death of Henry VII in 1509 resolved ll uncertainties with quite startling sudden-ess. Young Henry, a brisk and vigorous 18-ear-old, now master of his own life and uture, cut clean through the tangle of the receding six years by insisting that the mar-iage should take place as soon as it could be rranged. Whatever spurred Henry to action ust have been more for him than a coldly alculated act of statesmanship: contempo-ary accounts make it abundantly clear that e was greatly taken with his bride. She was ntelligent, accomplished, and spirited; a ore than suitable companion for a young nd energetic king.

The prime duty of any queen was to bear her husband's children, preferably sons, to ensure the continuity of the dynasty and an undisputed succession on his death. Cather-ine did her best and was far from barren. Twice she miscarried, once she was delivered of a stillborn girl; two sons died in early infancy, the one a few hours, the other a few weeks after birth; only one child survived – Princess Mary, who was born in 1516. Catherine's last recorded pregnancy was early in 1518. Henry became increasingly frus-trated and disappointed, and yet for 18 years he remained a devoted and comparatively loyal husband. Certainly he had affairs with other women, but only two can be named with any degree of confidence: Elizabeth Blount, who bore him a son, and Mary Boleyn, elder sister of the more famous Anne.

*LEFT:*
  *Henry at about the*
  *age of 30.*

*BELOW:*
  *A contemporary*
  *woodcut depicts the*
  *coronation of Henry*
  *and Catherine on 24*
  *June 1509.*

*BOTTOM:*
  *Catherine looks on*
  *while Henry jousts at*
  *a tournament held in*
  *celebration of the birth*
  *of a son in 1512, but*
  *the child died aged*
  *only a few weeks.*

In 1527 the 'King's Great Matter' first became public knowledge. By then it was quite clear that Catherine, now 42, was past the age of childbearing, while Henry, at 36, was still in his physical prime. He grew increasingly anxious about the succession, the security of which depended on Catherine's sole surviving child, Princess Mary, now aged 11. In 1525 Henry's son by Elizabeth Blount had been publicly acknowledged and given the title Duke of Richmond. This seemed to many to be a prelude to naming him as Henry's heir, a step that was never in fact taken, though from then until the young

> '**The Queen and I are both young and if it is a girl this time, by God's grace boys will follow.**'
>
> HENRY TO THE VENETIAN AMBASSADOR
> FOLLOWING THE BIRTH OF PRINCESS MARY

man's death in 1536 it was always a possibility. In 1527 Henry had also fallen victim to the charms of Anne Boleyn who seems to have made it clear that she would not yield to his advances until she was assured of status and security as his wife. These were the circumstances which combined to persuade Henry to take a critical look at his marriage and to 'discover' the text in Leviticus which seemed to point directly at him: 'If a man shall take his brother's wife it is an unclean thing . . . they shall be childless' (Leviticus XX, 21).

Henry and Catherine were not of course exactly childless, but a daughter was of little use to a king in a country where there was virtually no precedent for a woman ruler. God knew the needs of England and yet denied the king a son. This, thought Henry, could only be a divine judgement on his incestuous marriage.

And so began the long and sordid story of the attempt to secure an annulment of Henry's marriage to Catherine, by alleging the inadequacy of the bull of Pope Julius I upon which it rested.

LEFT:
*The impaled arms of
Henry VIII and
Catherine of Aragon.
Henry's Tudor rose is
shown while
Catherine is identified
by the pomegranate.*

From the very beginning Catherine was at a considerable disadvantage. At first she was kept in ignorance of what was afoot. Later, when the news leaked out, she was, for form's sake, given counsel, but counsel chosen for her by the king. It was also hoped in the beginning that the whole matter could be quickly settled in England by a specially appointed papal tribunal in which the king's chief minister, Cardinal Wolsey, would be one of the presiding judges; but Catherine boldly challenged the impartiality of such a court and appealed direct to the Pope. Even then she would have had little chance of a sympathetic hearing had it not been for the consistent and powerful support she received from her nephew, the Emperor Charles V.

For six long years the legal and political battle raged. Queen Catherine sought by every means to defend her name, her marriage, and the legitimacy of her child, but in 1533 King Henry lost patience. He rejected the authority of the Holy See, and got from his own archbishop, Thomas Cranmer, the decree of nullity which he had so long desired. But Catherine still held out, steadfastly refusing to abandon the title of queen or to adopt

the title 'Princess Dowager of Wales' which was now officially accorded her as one who was Arthur's widow but had never been Henry's wife.

Separated from her daughter, banished from the court, obliged to live in seclusion in a succession of damp, unhealthy castles and manors on the fringes of the fens, and deprived of all but a handful of faithful servants, Catherine spent her last few years in acute loneliness and sorrow. Yet she seldom complained and spent much time in prayer. She died at Kimbolton on 7 January 1536, three weeks after her 50th birthday, and was buried in Peterborough Abbey with such state as was appropriate to the widow of the Prince of Wales. Henry did not attend the funeral.

# Anne Boleyn

BORN 1502(?), MARRIED 1532/3, EXECUTED 1536

Very little is known for certain about Anne's early years, and even the date of her birth is disputed, although 1502 is the likeliest. She was the daughter of Sir Thomas Boleyn, a man of London merchant stock, who had successfully risen high in the social scale by marrying into the noble Howard family, and through her mother Anne was a niece of the Duke of Norfolk. Probably born at the family seat of Hever in Kent, Anne was, while still a child, sent to France for her education where, at the French court, under the eye of the French queen, she learned the accomplishments thought appropriate to a lady of breeding in her generation.

Some time in 1521 or early 1522, when war between England and France was imminent, Anne returned to England and came to the court of King Henry. Anne did not make any immediate impression on the king, though she seems to have cast quite a spell over some of the younger men and was about to be engaged to one of them when Cardinal Wolsey (perhaps acting on the king's instructions) stepped in to prevent it. Anne's sister, Mary, had earlier been the king's mistress, and although the dates and details of this liaison are obscure, many have seen the promotion of Sir Thomas Boleyn to the peerage as result of Mary's influence over Henry.

It is not easy more than four centuries later to appraise the qualities which enabled Anne to establish and maintain such a firm hold over the emotions of a headstrong monarch. Henry was not accustomed to having his immediate wants denied, and yet for nearly six years Anne kept him waiting until she could be assured of recognition as his wife and queen. What is often overlooked however, is that Henry had very good reasons for being prepared to wait. Privately he may have desired Anne for herself alone, but publicly he needed a son, and a son born in wedlock. To father further bastards would in

no way help to avoid that succession crisis which the king could see arising if he died without a legitimate son. His union with Anne must therefore be as regular and legitimate as he could make it. He was not to know at the outset how long the legal wranglings involved in securing his release from Catherine would take. Anne's charms must have been potent, and yet contemporary descriptions of her are far from flattering. However, in her brief career she made many enemies so the surviving record may well be coloured by spite. When Anne had been arrested and was soon to die, Henry complained of having been bewitched, but Anne

'magic' was probably nothing more than a bubbling vivacity and an ability to tease and tantalise.

The complicated proceedings of the 'King's Great Matter' began in 1527. At first Anne was kept discreetly in the background – to have paraded her too openly as his intended bride would have prejudiced his case and harmed his reputation, for Catherine was very popular with the people. But by 1530, as the affair dragged on, Anne was being openly honoured at court. Catherine was still present, though virtually ignored by Henry, and friction between her and her supplanter caused many an unpleasant scene. The next year Catherine was ordered to leave the court and Anne reigned supreme. In 1532 she was raised to the peerage in her own right as Marchioness of Pembroke and accompanied Henry on a state visit to France, although the ladies of the French court refused to meet her.

Henry's patience now gave out. In full accord with his unshakable conviction that he and Catherine had never been legally man and wife, he was married to his Anne, probably in mid-September 1532.

*LEFT:*
*Cardinal Thomas Wolsey supported Henry's divorce from Catherine of Aragon but he was still hated by Anne, who blamed him for the many delays in the divorce proceedings. Anne had another reason to hate Wolsey: some years before (probably acting under Henry's instructions) he had played a part in preventing an engagement between Anne and Lord Henry Percy, heir to the 5th Earl of Northumberland.*

*LEFT:*
*Hever Castle, Anne's family home and where, possibly, she was born in 1502. She certainly spent some of her childhood at Hever, and Henry visited her here occasionally during their long courtship, when they would stroll together in the grounds.*

*RIGHT:*

*A contemporary drawing of Greenwich Palace where Henry was born and spent much of his early life. It was the Tudors' maritime home and the scene of Anne Boleyn's downfall.*

*BELOW:*

*The impaled arms of Henry VIII and Anne Boleyn.*

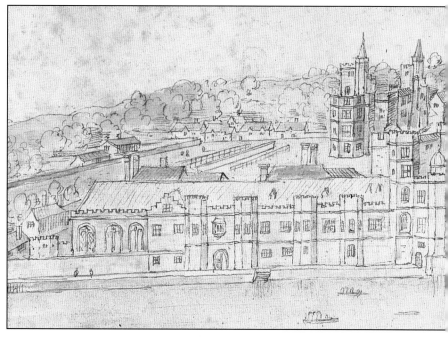

A great deal of mystery surrounds this particular wedding. Who performed it, where and precisely when it took place, and who were witnesses, we shall probably never know, for even Thomas Cranmer, who in May 1533 was to sit in judgement on the marriage and to pronounce it valid, betrays in a letter written only a few weeks later a surprising vagueness even about its date.

But more important to Henry was that by early 1533 it was known Anne was carrying his child. To ensure the legitimacy of the hoped-for heir their union must be regularised before the child's birth, and so events were hurried on. In January 1533 Thomas Cranmer was nominated to the see of Canterbury; in February the Pope confirmed his appointment, and in March he was consecrated and installed. Meanwhile Parliament had passed the Act in Restraint of Appeals which denied to the Pope any power to interfere in matrimonial cases arising in England, and in May Cranmer pronounced Henry's first marriage void and his second valid. On 1 June Anne, now openly accepted as Henry's wife, was crowned as queen. It was thus only necessary to await the birth of her child – confidently expected to be a boy – and Anne's triumph would be complete.

On 7 September 1533, however, Anne gave birth to a girl. No-one could then foresee the triumphant reign of the future Queen Elizabeth and so for Henry the potential succession crisis was still no nearer a solution. He made little attempt to conceal his disappointment and by 1535 it was obvious that Henry had tired of Anne. Only producing a

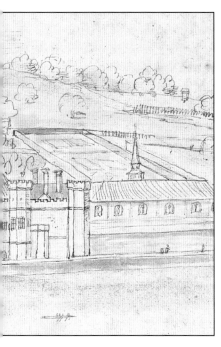

son could save her, but in January 1536, a few weeks after Catherine of Aragon's death, she miscarried of a son.

To Henry it seemed his second marriage was no better than his first. Perhaps there was a curse upon this marriage also. After all, Anne's sister Mary had been his mistress, and marriage with a sister of one's mistress was possibly as sinful in the eyes of God as marriage with one's brother's widow. The relationships were similar, and now, with Catherine dead, Anne was the only stumbling block between Henry and a third, perfectly regular and unquestionably valid marriage.

Even so, it is hard to understand Henry's total rejection of Anne whom he had once loved so passionately. It would have been quite sufficient either to have executed her or to have annulled the marriage, but Henry did both. Her own brother and four other courtiers were arrested and accused of having been intimate with her and of plotting to assassinate the king; under threat of torture one of them confessed, and it was enough to condemn them all. Anne went to the block on 19 May 1536, and her alleged paramours were shown no mercy. But two days before she died her marriage was dissolved and Henry was a bachelor once more. Anne's decapitated body was buried without ceremony in the Tower of London, and ten days later the king married again.

ABOVE:
The Family of Henry VIII, probably painted c.1545. The five main figures are, from the left, Princess Mary, Prince Edward, Henry VIII, his queen (almost certainly Jane Seymour) and Princess Elizabeth. This was not painted from life as Jane Seymour died days after Prince Edward's birth, but she is represented in the picture as the mother of the King's heir.

Princess
Mary

Henry Fitzroy
(illegitimate)

*Princess
Elizabeth*

*Prince
Edward*

# Jane Seymour

*RIGHT:*

*Holbein's portrait of Jane Seymour, Henry's third wife, is probably a true likeness. She was a quiet and gentle girl who did not immediately attract attention. Her father, Sir John Seymour of Wolf Hall in Wiltshire, was a knight of ancient but not very remarkable lineage.*

*RIGHT:*

*This portrait of Henry was painted in the year of his marriage to Jane. He was 45 years old.*

*BELOW:*

*Hampton Court Palace, where Prince Edward was born in October 1537 and where Jane died.*

*BELOW RIGHT:*

*The arms of Jane Seymour.*

Jane's career was in many ways similar to that of Anne Boleyn. Each was in turn lady-in-waiting to the queen she eventually supplanted, and each refused to entertain an illicit relationship with the king, insisting on recognition as wife and queen. Yet because Jane died so shortly after her great triumph, bearing the king his longed-for son, and because she retained his devotion right up to the moment of her death, she has generally been treated more kindly by posterity.

Jane's father, Sir John Seymour, was honoured for his services to Henry, and his position at court provided excellent opportunities for his family's advancement. Three of his eight children were to rise to fame: his eldest son Edward as Duke of Somerset and Lord

Protector during the minority of the boy-king Edward VI; his second son Thomas as lord admiral; and his eldest daughter Jane as Queen.

It is not known for certain when Jane first came to court. She was, it is thought, attached to the household of Queen Catherine, being transferred to the service of Anne Boleyn as the latter rose and the former fell. She seems to have been far less spirited than Anne, and Holbein's portrait of her is scarcely that of a dazzling charmer. In September 1535, almost two years to the day after the birth of Eliza-

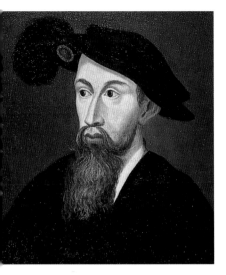

*We all hungered after a prince so long that there was as much rejoicing as at the birth of John the Baptist.*

BISHOP LATIMER

beth, the king stayed for a few days at Wolf Hall. However, if it was on this occasion that the king first really noticed Jane, the affair was slow to develop, for we hear no mention of his new love until February of the following year, 1536, when speculation began about the chances of Jane becoming queen.

By then Queen Anne was clearly in danger for cold indifference had replaced Henry's former infatuation. For Jane it was a somewhat dangerous honour to be the chosen consort of a strong-willed monarch who had defied pope and emperor to rid himself of one queen and was even now planning to rid himself of a second. Yet Jane impressed all who knew her with her calmness and gentleness, and she probably never really understood the political game in which she was deeply involved.

Anne was arrested and condemned and on 19 May 1536 she was executed. Henry and Jane were married less than two weeks later. Jane was never actually crowned queen, perhaps because Henry wished to be certain of the successful outcome of this marriage before he took the final step: his need to have a legitimate heir was now more urgent than ever, especially when on 23 July 1536 his only illegitimate son, the 17-year-old Henry Fitzroy, Duke of Richmond, died.

Rumours of the queen's pregnancy were confirmed in the early months of 1537 and at last, early in October, in the 29th year of

Henry's reign, Prince Edward was born, a son and heir of undoubted legitimacy.

On 15 October the baby was christened. Princess Mary, Catherine's daughter, now reconciled with her father, was godmother, and Princess Elizabeth, Anne's child, aged four, had her own part to play in the elaborate ceremonial. Queen Jane, though still very weak, was also present. It was a happy occasion but tragedy was not far away. Jane did not recover from what had been apparently a prolonged labour, and there are some grounds for supposing that her son was finally delivered by Caesarian section. Queen Jane died on 24 October 1537.

Her body was laid to rest in the tomb which Henry was already having prepared for himself at Windsor, and she is the only one of his wives to share his grave.

*ABOVE:*
*Twenty-nine years after Henry succeeded to the throne, Jane gave birth to the son he so desperately needed.*

*ABOVE LEFT:*
*Sir Edward Seymour, Jane's brother. On Henry's death he was created Lord Protector to his nephew the young King Edward VI.*

# Anne of Cleves

*RIGHT:*
*Anne of Cleves,*
*Henry's fourth wife.*
*This fine portrait by*
*Holbein does not*
*justify Henry's*
*description of her as a*
*'Flanders mare' and*
*she compares very*
*favourably in*
*appearance with her*
*predecessor Jane.*

Henry remained without a wife for more than two years after the death of Jane Seymour, but barely a month had passed before discreet enquiries were being made at both the French and the Imperial courts. These first feelers may of course have been put out without the king's knowledge by his ever-busy first minister, Thomas Cromwell. Since the break with Rome, England stood dangerously isolated in Europe, and the chance of using the king's availability to effect an alliance with one or other of the major western powers was too good an opportunity to miss. However even Cromwell would not have dared to initiate such enquiries without first receiving some positive indication of the king's approval.

*RIGHT:*
*King Henry VIII*
*dressed in the splendid*
*clothes he had made*
*for his wedding to*
*Anne of Cleves. It is*
*fairly clear that at the*
*very moment he*
*married Anne he was*
*already searching*
*round for ways to*
*free himself from all*
*his obligations*
*towards her.*

## 'I am ashamed that men have so praised her... and I like her not'

KING HENRY VIII

It seemed fairly clear from the start that Henry's next marriage would not be a love match with a lady of his own court, but an orthodox international affair in which diplomatic considerations would be every bit as important as personal. Yet the personal preferences of the English king could not be overlooked. He had strong views on the subject of female beauty and he insisted very firmly that his next wife must be personally pleasing to him. He took the greatest care not to let official advances be made in his name until he had had some means of satisfying himself that the lady in question would come up to his expectations. Agents secretly observed and commented upon the appearance, accomplishments and character of various potential brides. Court painters, including Holbein, travelled abroad to catch their likeness.

1538 passed by without positive progress being made with any of the king's potential courtships and then, by the end of the year, a political danger had arisen: the King of France and the Emperor had made up their long-standing quarrel and Henry feared they might join forces against England in support of the papal cause.

The combined principalities of Cleves, Julich, Mark and Berg, lying astride the lower Rhine, formed one of the up-and-coming states in Germany. The young duke was allied by marriage with Saxony and the league of Lutheran princes, and he was in dispute with the Emperor over the title to the Duchy of Gelderland. An alliance with Cleves would save England from total isolation – and, conveniently, the duke had two unmarried sisters. Holbein was sent to paint both Anne, aged 24, and her sister Amelia, and the king's interest was aroused. A marriage contract was drawn up between Henry and Anne, but even before it was concluded the Emperor and the King of France had returned to their normal state of enmity, and no longer posed a threat to Henry.

And yet the marriage still went ahead on 6 January 1540, with Henry already searching for ways to extricate himself. War between the Emperor and the Duke of Cleves was now on the cards and Henry had no intention of letting his obligation to Cleves involve him in hostilities against the Emperor. Anne was also very ill equipped for life in the sophisticated English court. She had been brought up in the restricted circle of the ducal court at Düsseldorf, her education having concentrated on domestic skills, and she was unfamiliar with the world of books and music, one of Henry's joys. Thus there were both political and personal reasons for wanting to be rid of Anne and the now inconvenient alliance she represented – and Catherine Howard had appeared on the scene.

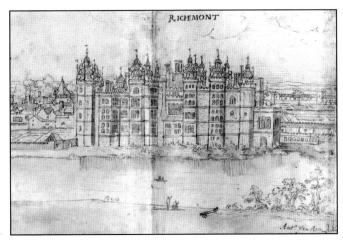

*'My Lord, if it were not to satisfy the world and my realm,*
*I would not do that I must do this day for none earthly thing'*

It took six months to untie the knot. The story of Henry's revulsion from the 'Flanders Mare', as Anne became known, rests almost exclusively on the recollections of courtiers anxious to support Henry's case for annulment, on the grounds of non-consummation. Henry also tried to prove that Anne's previous engagement to the son of the Duke of Lorraine had not been properly repudiated and stood as a legal bar to her marriage with Henry. Throughout the whole shabby affair Anne was most cooperative. She placed no obstacles in Henry's way, obediently producing the testimony he needed, and apparently content to accept the honorary title of 'King's sister', with the houses and lands that were her compensation. She retired to live in comfortable obscurity until 1557, surviving her royal 'brother' by more than a decade.

*ABOVE:*
*Richmond Palace. Anne retired here quietly after Henry divorced her.*

*LEFT:*
*Thomas Cromwell, Henry's chief secretary from 1533. Politically the King of England was the most eligible bachelor of his day and the problem of finding him a suitable fourth wife aroused keen interest all around Europe. Cromwell managed the negotiations and selected Anne of Cleves for diplomatic reasons.*

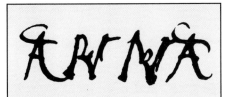

# Catherine Howard

*BELOW:*
*Catherine was Henry's 'very jewel of womanhood' but the dream did not last.*

*RIGHT:*
*Thomas Howard, third Duke of Norfolk, uncle to both Anne Boleyn and Catherine Howard. Although it is probably an exaggeration to claim that Catherine was deliberately paraded in front of Henry, once Henry's interest was aroused, the Duke of Norfolk clearly gave Catherine advice on how to play her hand.*

*RIGHT:*
*Henry was nearly fifty by the time he married the 19-year-old Catherine, and frequently referred to himself as an 'old man'.*

Catherine Howard was a gay, high-spirited girl, free with her favours and uninhibited in her behaviour. Her father, Lord Edmund Howard, was the ne'er-do-well younger brother of the Duke of Norfolk and she was a first cousin of Anne Boleyn. Catherine was brought up in the household of her step-grandmother, the dowager Duchess of Norfolk, widow of the victor of Flodden, and her earlier years were divided between Horsham and Lambeth, the principal residences of the duchess.

Henry's interest in her was aroused shortly after she gained entry to court, at the age of 19, as a lady-in-waiting to the new queen, Anne of Cleves. With Henry's latest marriage proving to be both politically and personally unsatisfactory, no doubt the tantalising presence of this latest bright-eyed charmer accelerated his disillusionment. Had the king not taken a fancy to her she would probably have been married off to some aspiring social climber to whom the satisfaction of marrying into one of the foremost noble houses of the

day would have been adequate compensation for the inadequacy of her dowry. She would undoubtedly have led any husband a dance and would probably have featured quite frequently in scandalous tales at court. But what might have been tolerated in the career of a minor court personage could not be permitted in a queen, who must be totally above suspicion.

Thomas Cromwell, for so long the first man in the kingdom, had been closely associated with the Cleves marriage from its first inception. Now his enemies at court, who included Catherine's uncle, Thomas Howard, Duke of Norfolk, saw in the king's dissatisfaction with Anne a chance to pull him down, and it is quite clear that once Henry's interest had been caught Catherine was carefully coached by her ambitious relatives. Henry and Catherine were married on 28 July 1540,

just 16 days after the nullification of his marriage to Anne of Cleves, while the unfortunate Cromwell was disgraced and executed.

For almost a year this strange marriage of opposites was a marked success. Henry, now nearly 50 years of age, had lost most of his youthful vigour and was severely handicapped by increasing corpulence and an ulcerated leg, and yet for a while he miraculously recovered a lot of his former zest for fe. The young queen, his 'very jewel of womanhood', was patently adored by her delighted spouse, who showered her with gifts and favours and pampered her in every way – and Catherine revelled in it. The gay whirl of court festivities was heaven to her and she had the youth and vigour to enjoy it to the full. The loving caresses of her ageing and obese husband may not have thrilled her quite so much but she took pleasure in the powers and privileges that belonged to her as queen.

But the dream was not to last. By April or May 1541 there were disturbing signs of growing tension. It was almost inevitable that Catherine should seek the company of young men her own age but foolish of her not to realise that even the most innocent of flirtations would be misrepresented by enemies at court. It was dangerous enough to use her patronage to appoint a former admirer as her private secretary but fatal to play at back-stairs intrigue with a handsome young man-about-court. By September 1541, when the king and court set out on an extended progress to the north, rumours were being whispered at court, and, early in November, immediately after the king's return to Hampton Court, sufficient evidence for the queen's misconduct had come to light to make Archbishop Cranmer feel he must inform the king.

Henry's immediate reaction was one of total disbelief. However, he ordered that enquiries be made, and the further the investigators probed the more damning the evidence they unearthed. Not only had Catherine been flirting wantonly behind her royal husband's back, it was alleged she had also been promiscuously unchaste before he married her. Henry was shattered. His much idealised young wife was revealed as an unscrupulous deceiver who had played with his affections and dishonoured his crown, and there could be no mercy. Catherine went the way of her cousin Anne Boleyn; she was tried and condemned, and on 13 February 1542 she was beheaded at the Tower of London.

*ABOVE:*
*The Queen's House at the Tower of London where Catherine was held before her execution.*

*BELOW LEFT:*
*It is said that Catherine's ghost has been heard at the Haunted Gallery, Hampton Court.*

*BELOW:*
*The site of the scaffold.*

### Henry vowed he would cut off her head with his own sword.

# Catherine Parr

## BORN 1512, MARRIED 1543, DIED 1548

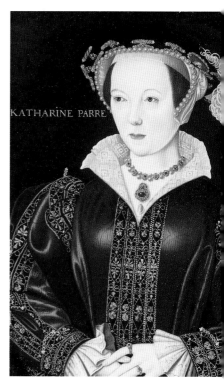

KATHARINE PARRE

For his sixth and last venture into matrimony, Henry was content to choose a rather different bride. Not for him this time a girl just barely out of her teens, but a woman of 31 who had already been twice widowed.

Very little is known of Catherine Parr's early life and upbringing, but this is not at all unusual in an age when even royal infancies are frequently inadequately documented. She was the daughter of Sir Thomas Parr of Kendal, a country squire of modest competence who had a very profitable and successful career in the royal service in the reigns of Henry VII and Henry VIII. Before his death in 1517, when Catherine was about five years old, he had risen to be controller of the Royal

Household. Catherine's mother did not remarry but apparently devoted herself to the education and advancement of her children. Catherine's brother, William, found favour at court and was eventually promoted to the peerage as Marquess of Northampton in 1547. Catherine, well schooled in Latin, Greek and French, became one of a small group of educated ladies at court who could debate confidently with the leading scholars of their day.

Catherine's first marriage, to Sir Edward Burough, was undistinguished and short-lived and, still in her teens, she was widowed in 1529. Catherine's mother also died at about this time, but it was not long before the young orphaned widow found a second husband in Sir John Nevill, Lord Latimer of Snape Hall in Yorkshire, a prominent landowner. In 1536 rebellion broke out in the north and Sir John found himself forced, like many of his Yorkshire neighbours, to lead the rebels. By participating in the rising Lord Latimer clearly ran the risk of capture and execution as a traitor, yet if he did not do as the rebels ordered is house would be burnt and his wife and family turned out. In the event he was among those who received the royal pardon and survived to die a natural death in 1542. He had no children by Catherine, but only by his two earlier wives.

By the time of her second widowhood Lady Latimer had become well known and much admired in court circles for her learning and accomplishments. She was also possessed of a sensitivity and sympathetic feeling which was exceptional in a court where tension between the rival religious groups and between the ambitious younger men and the established older men was becoming increasingly acute and the parties jostled and manoeuvred for position around the visibly ageing king. It is clear from her later actions that Catherine's personal sympathies lay with the protestant faction, but she was far too careful to reveal this openly while Henry was still alive.

Henry's courtship of Catherine is not well documented. Nearly 18 months elapsed between the execution of Catherine Howard and the marriage of the king to Catherine Parr on 12 July 1543. By the 1540s Henry's

infirmities were undermining his accustomed vigour and he seems to have been in no hurry to get married again. When he did marry Catherine she became as much a nurse to him as a wife. She knew well how to humour him, how to deflect his increasingly arbitrary wrath, how to ease his pain and soothe his spirits. Life with this irascible man-mountain in his declining years cannot have been easy. Yet Catherine managed to bring to the intimate circle of the royal family a degree of harmony and mutual affection it had scarcely ever known before. The two princesses, Mary and Elizabeth, were reconciled with their father and encouraged in their studies. Young Edward's education, at the age of seven, was committed to the care of two of the most able scholars of the day. Even Anne of Cleves, the king's 'sister', was made to feel at home.

*ABOVE:*

*Thomas Cranmer, Archbishop of Canterbury. In July 1543 he issued a licence stating that the marriage of Henry and Catherine Parr could take place in any church or chapel without the need for the publication of the banns.*

*LEFT:*

*The young Prince Edward. Catherine ensured he had only the best tutors.*

*BELOW:*

*Thomas Seymour, brother of Jane Seymour. Catherine rejected Thomas's proposal of marriage in order to accept the king, but they did not forget each other and were eventually free to marry.*

*BELOW RIGHT:*

*Sudeley Castle, Gloucestershire, home of the Seymour family. After her marriage to Thomas Seymour, Catherine lived here, together with her stepdaughter Princess Elizabeth, until she died in 1548.*

All this domestic harmony was achieved by Catherine at some considerable personal cost. Just before Henry had declared his intentions to her she had been actively sought in marriage by the younger of the Seymours, Thomas, uncle of Prince Edward and brother of the late Queen Jane. It was duty rather than affection that made her reject Seymour and accept the king. But Seymour did not forget her, nor she him. When Henry died in January 1547 and Catherine was free once more, she and Seymour were secretly married and braved the disapproval of the elder Seymour, the Lord Protector, Somerset.

As queen, Catherine had her enemies, jealous of her influence with the king. More than once they tried to turn him against her, alleging that she was in league with dangerous heretics and would-be innovators in religion. But every time her meekness and submission to her royal husband saved the day and Catherine lived to survive her spouse.

Catherine's failure to bear Henry a child was not apparently a source of danger to her as it had been to so many of her predecessors. The king seems at long last to have been content to accept that in two daughters and a son he had made as good provision as he could for the future of his throne and realm.

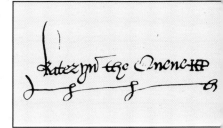

That Catherine was not herself to blame for the unfruitfulness of her first three marriages was made quite clear when she gave birth to Thomas Seymour's child on 30 August 1548. But, like her sister-in-law and predecessor as queen, Jane Seymour, she did not long survive the birth. She died on 7 September and was buried at the Seymour manor of Sudeley.

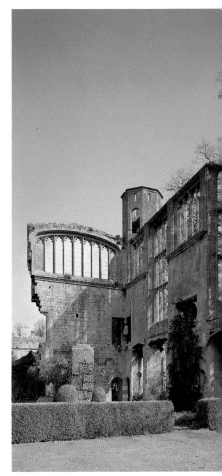